Baby

cross stitch
Cute Baby Models

Lesley Teare

Project Gallery

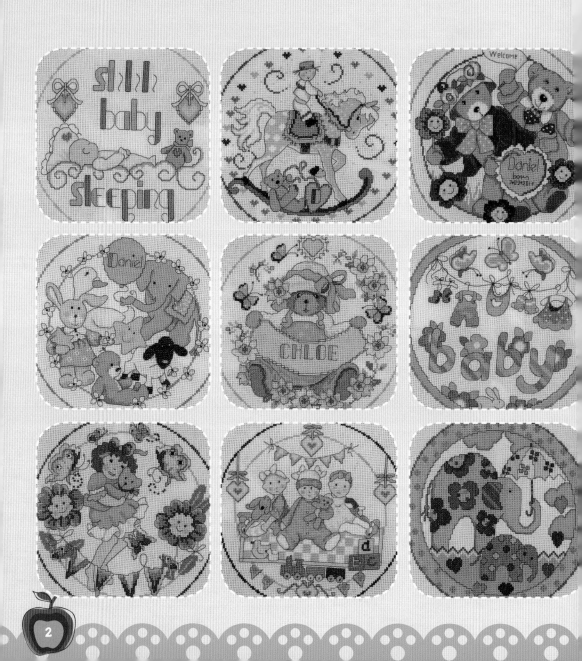

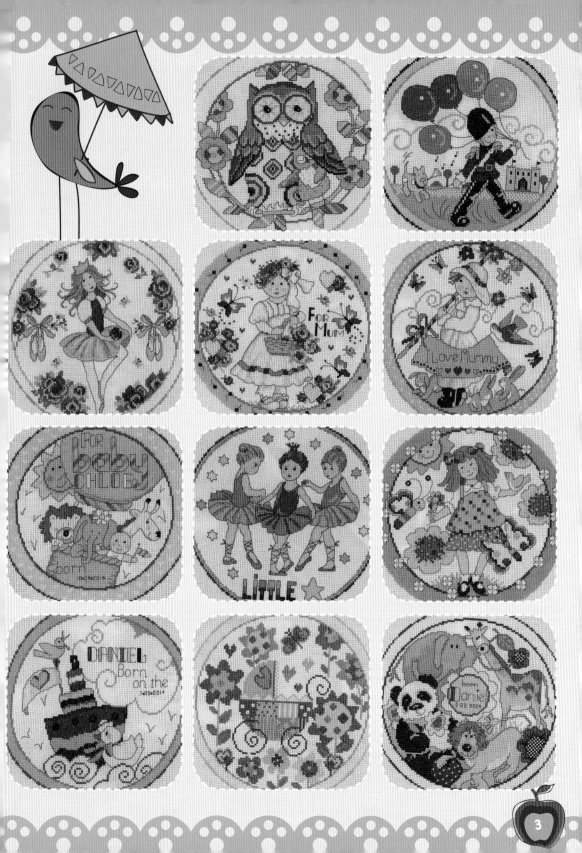

Project1

still baby sleeping

baby sleeping

Project 2

DMC
Mouliné
Stranded Cotton Art. 117

::	B5200
▽▽	209
∫∫	310
▲▲	434
++	436
UU	444
⊙⊙	445
<<	564
↑↑	603
€€	605
	818
○○	3827
——	844

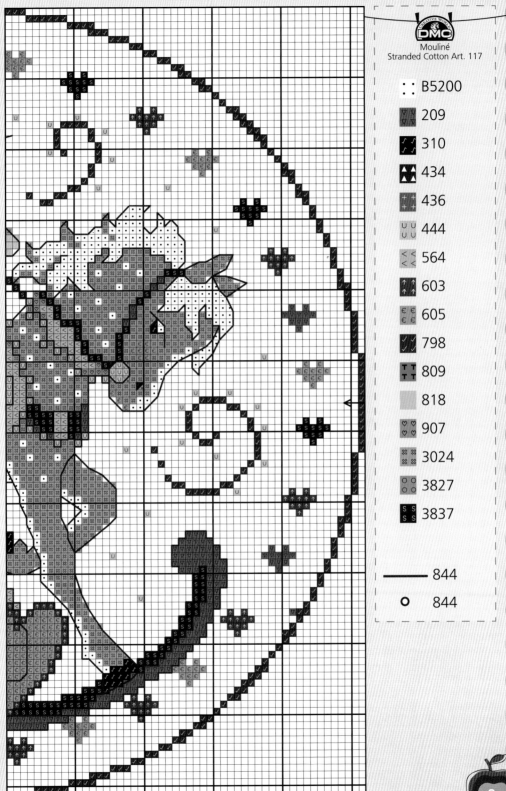

DMC
Mouliné
Stranded Cotton Art. 117

∵	B5200
🔲	209
◿	310
▲▲	434
++	436
U U	444
<<	564
↑↑	603
€ €	605
✓✓	798
T T	809
	818
♡♡	907
※※	3024
O O	3827
S S	3837

——	844
O	844

Project 3

Welcome

Daniel
born
7•09•2014

10

Project 4

11

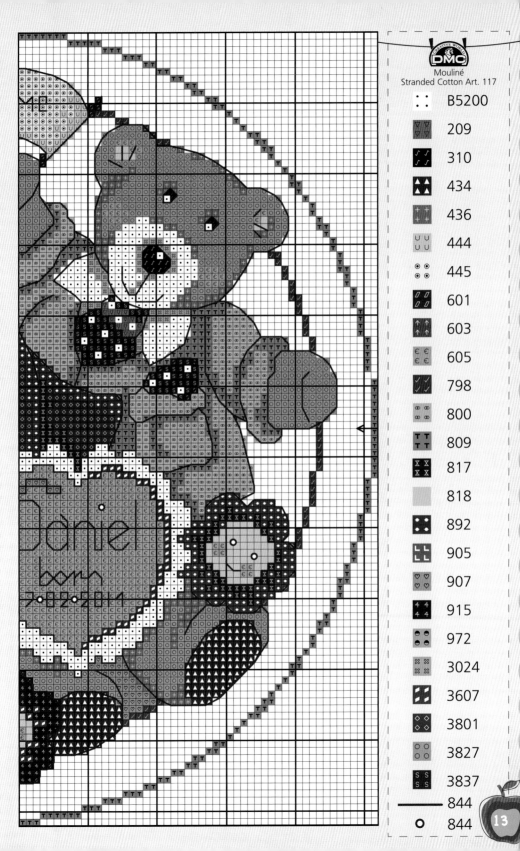

DMC
Mouliné
Stranded Cotton Art. 117

::	B5200
∀∀	209
⌁⌁	310
▲▲	434
++	436
UU	444
◉◉	445
⊘⊘	601
↑↑	603
€€	605
✓✓	798
∞∞	800
TT	809
XX	817
	818
∷∷	892
LL	905
♡♡	907
44	915
◖◖	972
⌘⌘	3024
♫♫	3607
◇◇	3801
○○	3827
SS	3837
——	844
O	844

13

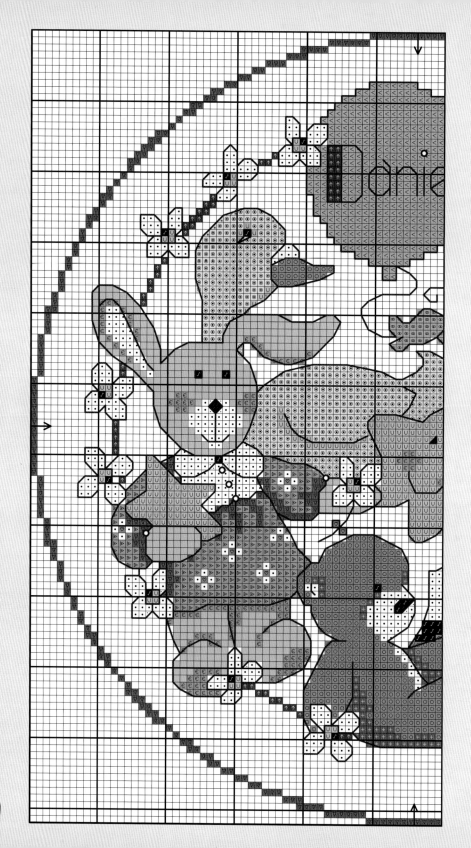

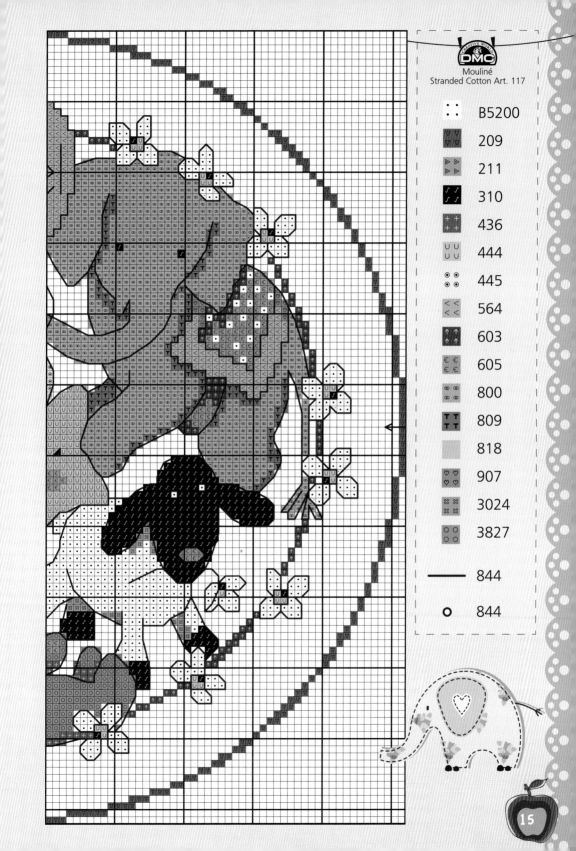

Mouliné
Stranded Cotton Art. 117

::	B5200
∀∀	209
▷▷	211
♪♪	310
++	436
UU	444
⊙⊙	445
<<	564
↑↑	603
€€	605
∞∞	800
TT	809
	818
♡♡	907
✕✕	3024
○○	3827
——	844
O	844

Project 5

CHLOE

Project 6

baby

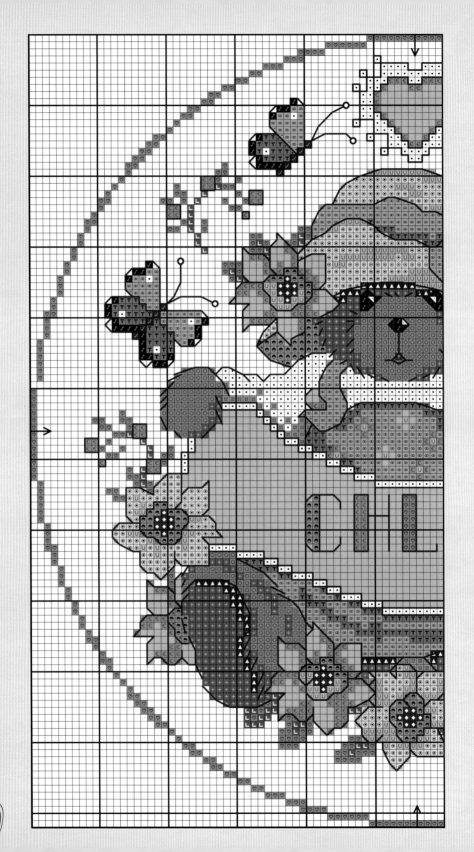

DMC
Mouliné
Stranded Cotton Art. 117

::	B5200
	209
	310
	434
	436
U U	444
° °	445
< <	564
↑ ↑	603
ϵ ϵ	605
	798
∞ ∞	800
T T	809
	818
L L	905
♥ ♥	907
	947
	972
	3024
○ ○	3827
———	844
O	844

19

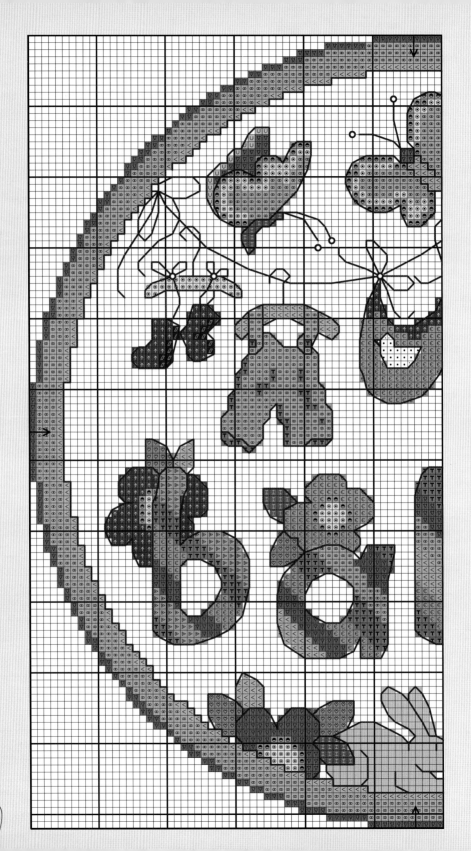

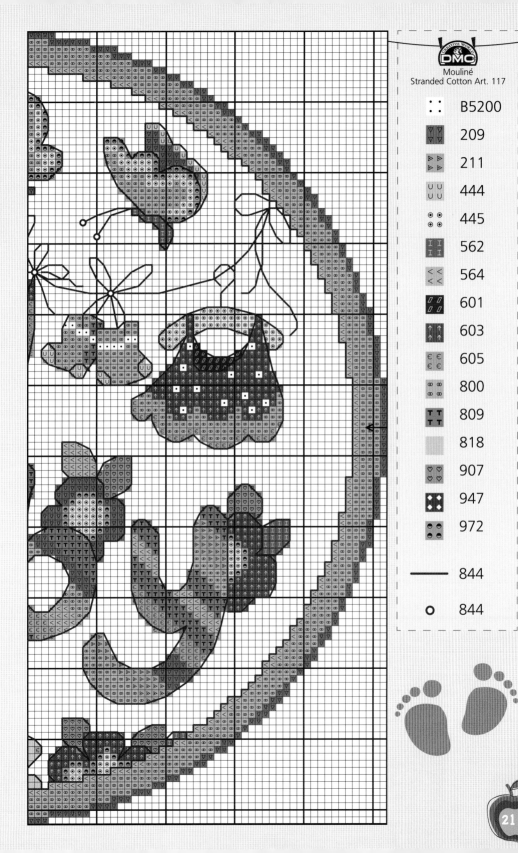

DMC
Mouliné
Stranded Cotton Art. 117

Symbol	Code
::	B5200
∇∇	209
▷▷	211
UU	444
◦◦	445
II	562
<<	564
∥∥	601
↑↑	603
€€	605
∞∞	800
TT	809
	818
♡♡	907
✦✦	947
●●	972
——	844
o	844

Project 7

DMC
Mouliné
Stranded Cotton Art. 117

Symbol	Color
: :	B5200
∇∇ /	209
▷▷ ▷▷	211
∫∫	310
▲▲	434
+ +	436
U U U	444
◦ ◦	445
I I	562
< <	564
∅ ∅	601
↑ ↑	603
ε ε	605
✓ ✓	798
∞ ∞	800
T T T T	809
	818
♡ ♡	907
● ●	972
⊠ ⊠	3024
▦ ▦	3607
◦ ◦	3827
S S S S	3837
——	844
○	844

25

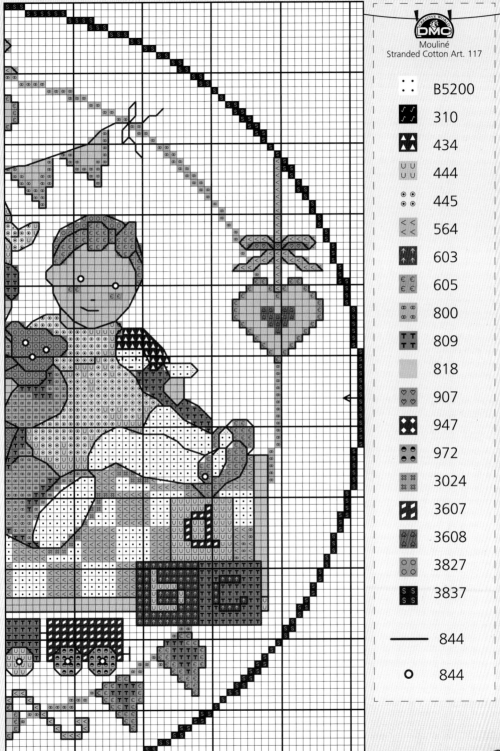

DMC
Mouliné
Stranded Cotton Art. 117

::	B5200
✓✓	310
▲▲	434
U U	444
⊙ ⊙	445
< <	564
↑↑	603
€ €	605
∞ ∞	800
T T	809
	818
♡♡	907
✖✖	947
●●	972
⁂ ⁂	3024
⁄⁄	3607
◢◢	3608
○ ○	3827
S S	3837
——	844
O	844

27

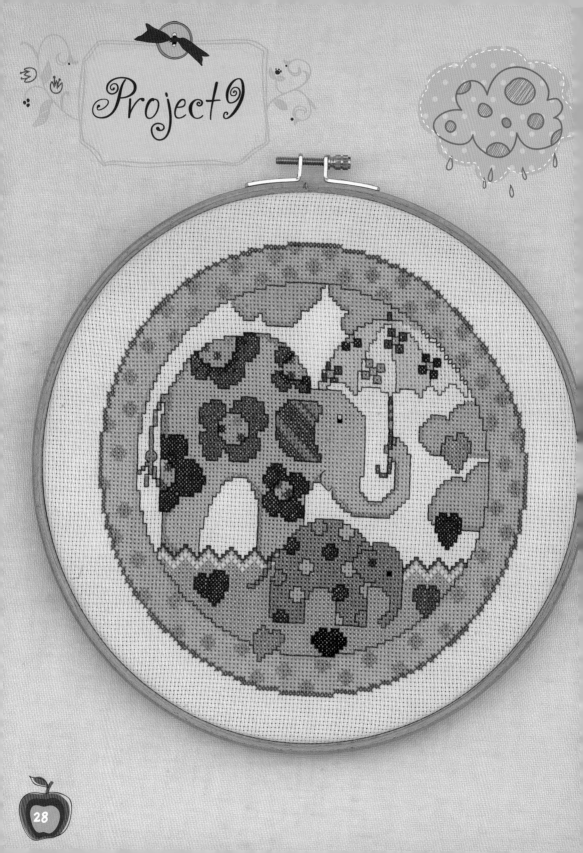

Project 9

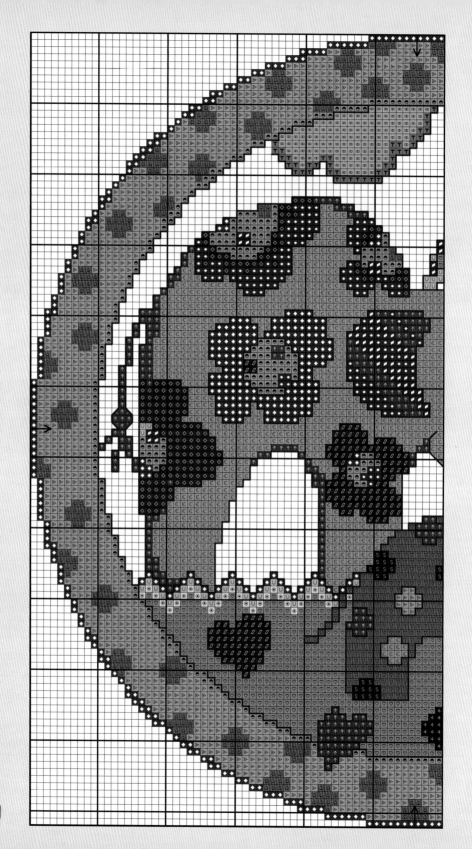

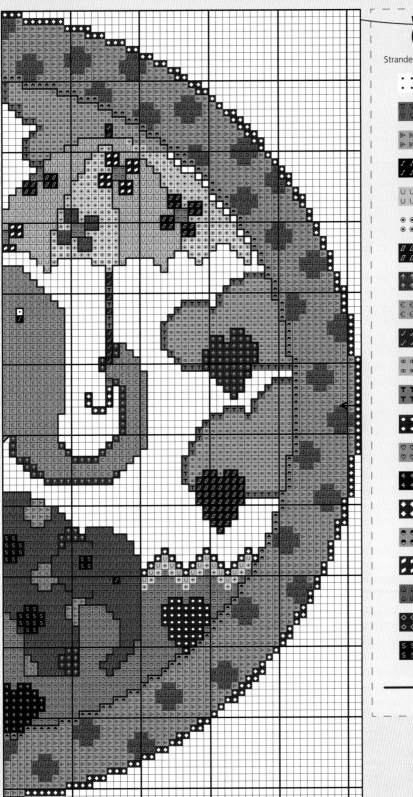

DMC
Mouliné
Stranded Cotton Art. 117

Symbol	Color
::	B5200
▼	209
▷▷	211
∫∫	310
U U	444
⊙⊙	445
∥∥	601
↑↑	603
€€	605
✓✓	798
∞∞	800
T T	809
■■	892
♡♡	907
4 4	915
✕✕	947
●●	972
◪◪	3607
◣◣	3608
◇◇	3801
S S	3837
——	844

31

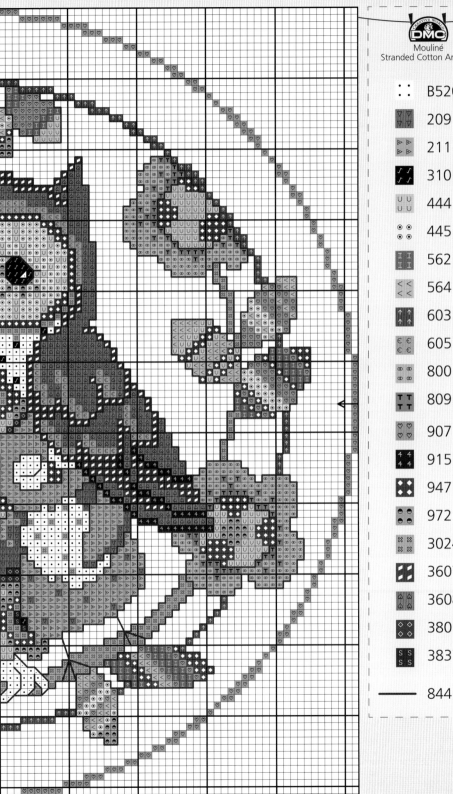

Mouliné
Stranded Cotton Art. 117

::	B5200
∀∀	209
▷▷	211
✗✗	310
U U	444
◉◉	445
I I	562
<<	564
↑↑	603
∈∈	605
∞∞	800
T T	809
♡♡	907
4 4	915
◆◆	947
●●	972
⊠⊠	3024
◗◗	3607
♠♠	3608
◇◇	3801
S S	3837
——	844

33

Project 11

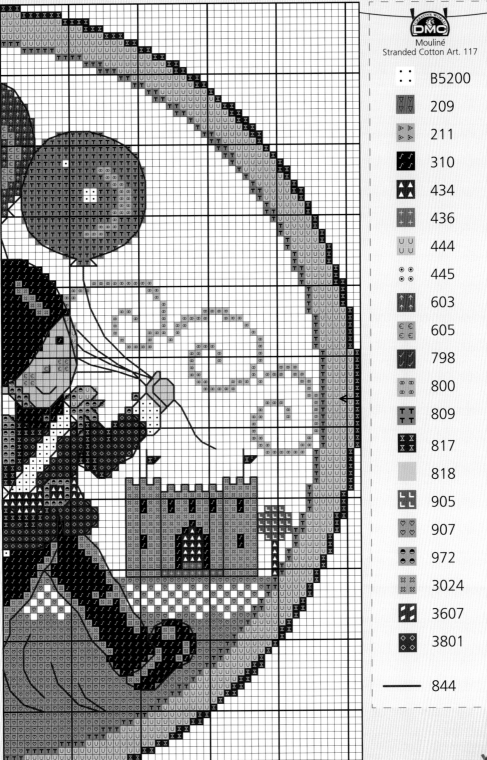

DMC
Mouliné
Stranded Cotton Art. 117

Symbol	Code
::	B5200
▽▽	209
▷▷	211
∿	310
▲▲	434
++	436
UU	444
⊚⊚	445
↑↑	603
€€	605
✓✓	798
∞∞	800
TT	809
XX	817
	818
⌐⌐	905
♡♡	907
●●●●	972
⊠⊠	3024
⧛⧛	3607
◇◇	3801
——	844

37

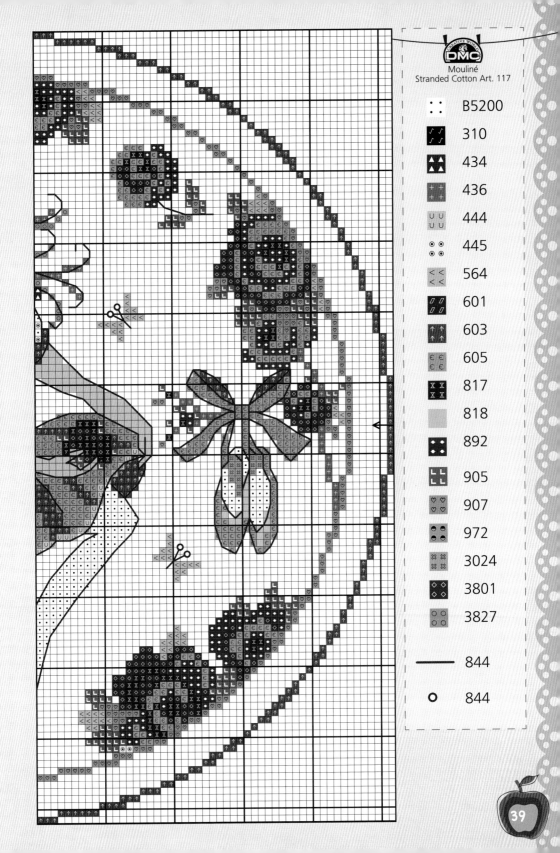

Mouliné
Stranded Cotton Art. 117

Symbol	Color
∴ ∴	B5200
∫∫	310
▲▲	434
++	436
U U U	444
◉ ◉	445
< <	564
◻◻	601
↑↑	603
ℰℰ	605
X X	817
	818
∷ ∷	892
L L	905
♡ ♡	907
●●	972
⧗⧗	3024
◇ ◇	3801
○ ○	3827
——	844
○	844

For Mum

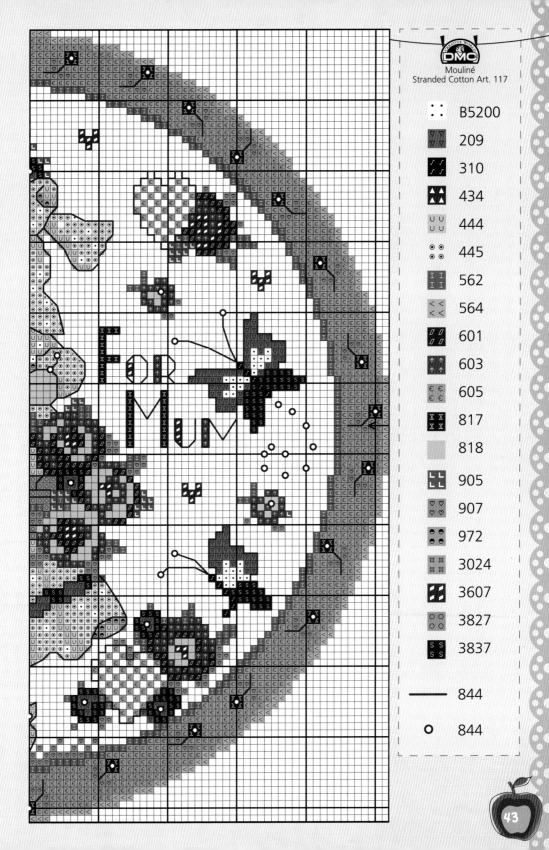

DMC
Mouliné
Stranded Cotton Art. 117

Symbol	Colour
: :	B5200
▼▼	209
∫∫	310
▲▲	434
U U	444
◉◉	445
I I	562
< <	564
◢◢	601
↑↑	603
€ €	605
X X	817
	818
L L	905
♥♥	907
●●	972
✕✕	3024
⧗⧗	3607
○○	3827
S S	3837
——	844
O	844

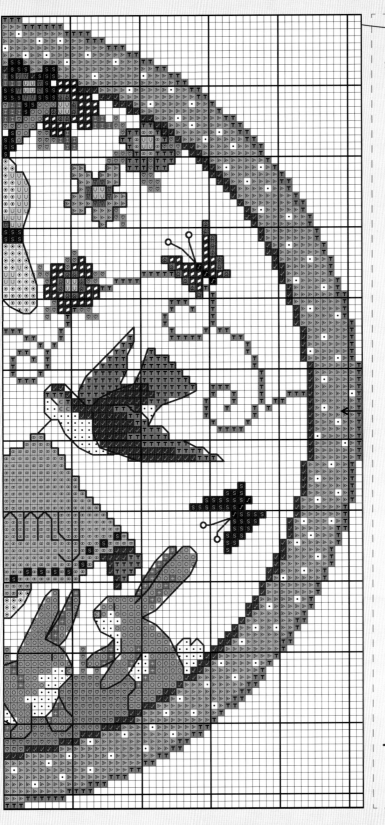

DMC CREATIVE WORLD

Mouliné
Stranded Cotton Art. 117

Symbol	Color
::	B5200
ⅤⅤ	209
▷▷	211
∫∫	310
▲▲	434
++	436
UU	444
⊙⊙	445
ⅠⅠ	562
00	601
€€	605
✓✓	798
∞∞	800
⊤⊤	809
	818
♡♡	907
●●	972
⊠⊠	3024
▌▌	3607
♠♠	3608
◇◇	3801
○○	3827
ƨƨ	3837
——	844
○	844

For baby
Chloe

little

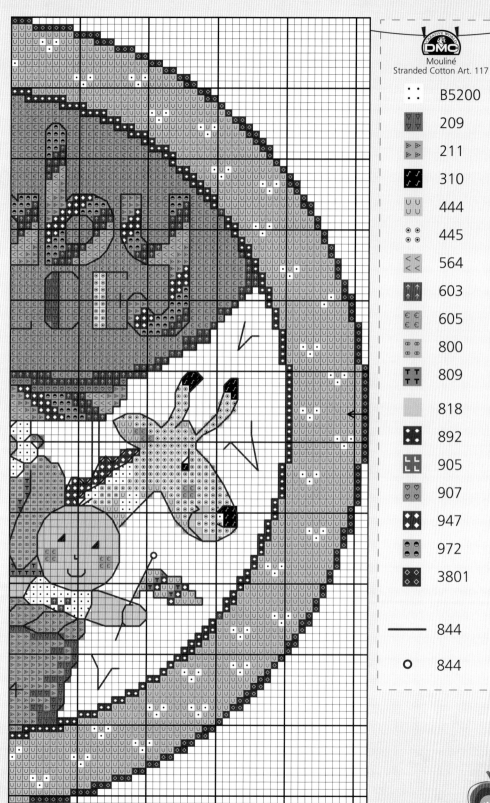

DMC
Mouliné
Stranded Cotton Art. 117

∵∴	B5200
▽▽▽	209
▷▷▷	211
⌇⌇	310
U U U	444
⊙⊙	445
< < <	564
↑↑	603
€ € € € € €	605
∞∞	800
T T T T	809
	818
⬛	892
L L L L	905
♡♡ ♡♡	907
⬛	947
●●	972
◇◇	3801
———	844
○	844

49

DMC
Mouliné
Stranded Cotton Art. 117

▽▽	209
▷▷	211
♩♩	310
▲▲	434
++	436
UU	444
◦◦	445
⊘⊘	601
↑↑	603
€€	605
	818
44	915
●●	972
	3607
♠♠	3608
◌◌	3827
SS	3837
——	844

Project 17

Project18

DANIEL
Born
on the
7·02·2014

53

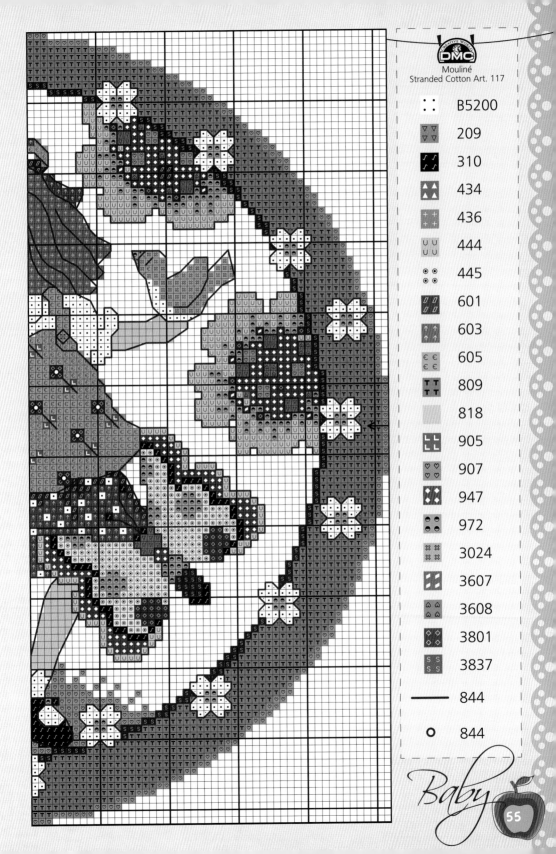

DMC

Mouliné
Stranded Cotton Art. 117

Symbol	Code
::	B5200
▽▽	209
⌡⌡	310
▲▲	434
++	436
U U	444
◉◉	445
⃫⃫	601
↑↑	603
∈∈	605
T T	809
	818
L L	905
♡♡	907
⧓⧓	947
◕◕	972
⋇⋇	3024
⧗⧗	3607
⌂⌂	3608
◇◇	3801
S S	3837
—	844
O	844

Baby

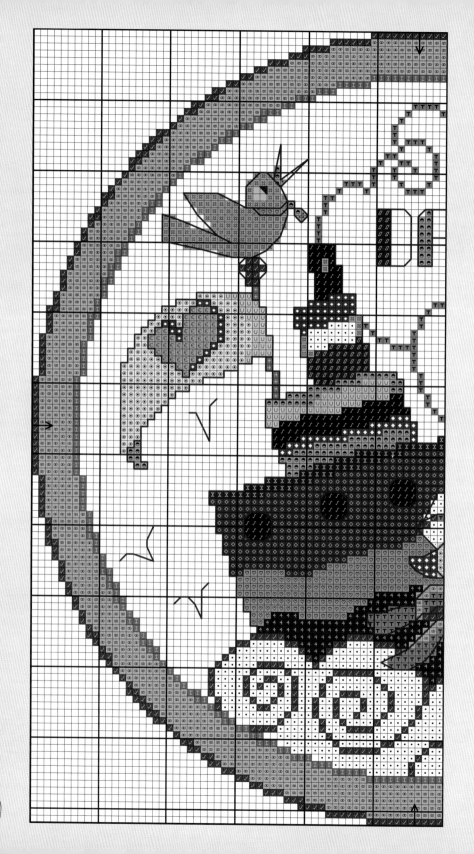

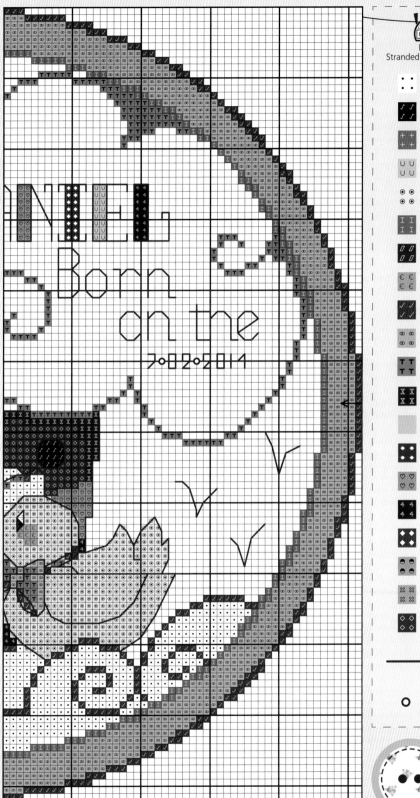

DMC
Mouliné
Stranded Cotton Art. 117

Symbol	Color
: :	B5200
ʃ ʃ	310
+ +	436
U U	444
◦ ◦	445
I I	562
◻ ◻	601
€ €	605
✓ ✓	798
⊚ ⊚	800
T T	809
X X	817
	818
▪ ▪	892
♡ ♡	907
4 4	915
▪ ▪	947
▪ ▪	972
▨ ▨	3024
◇ ◇	3801
——	844
o	844

Project 19

Project 20

DMC
Mouliné
Stranded Cotton Art. 117

::	B5200
▽▽	209
▷▷	211
U U	444
◦◦	445
I I	562
⬚⬚	601
↑↑	603
€€	605
::	892
LL	905
♡♡	907
✖✖	947
●●	972
⬛⬛	3607
◈◈	3608
◇◇	3801
SS	3837

62

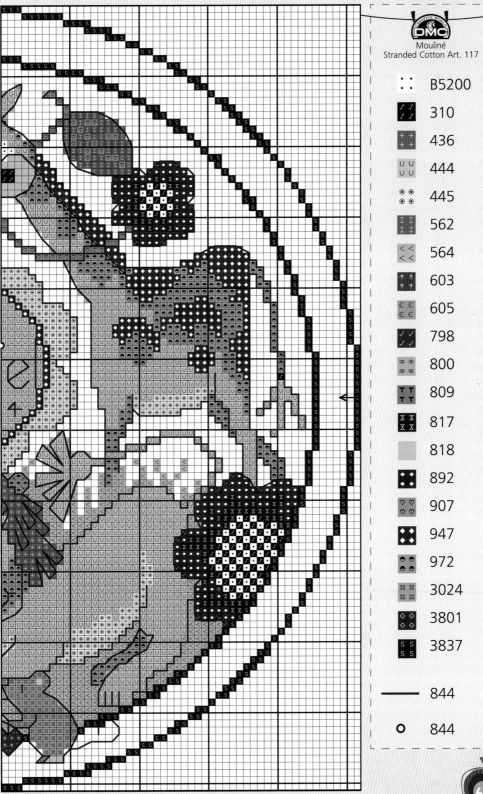

DMC

Mouliné
Stranded Cotton Art. 117

::	B5200
∫∫	310
++	436
UU	444
∘∘	445
II	562
<<	564
↑↑	603
∈∈	605
✓✓	798
∞∞	800
TT	809
XX	817
	818
■■	892
♡♡	907
■■	947
●●	972
⊠⊠	3024
◇◇	3801
ss	3837
———	844
O	844

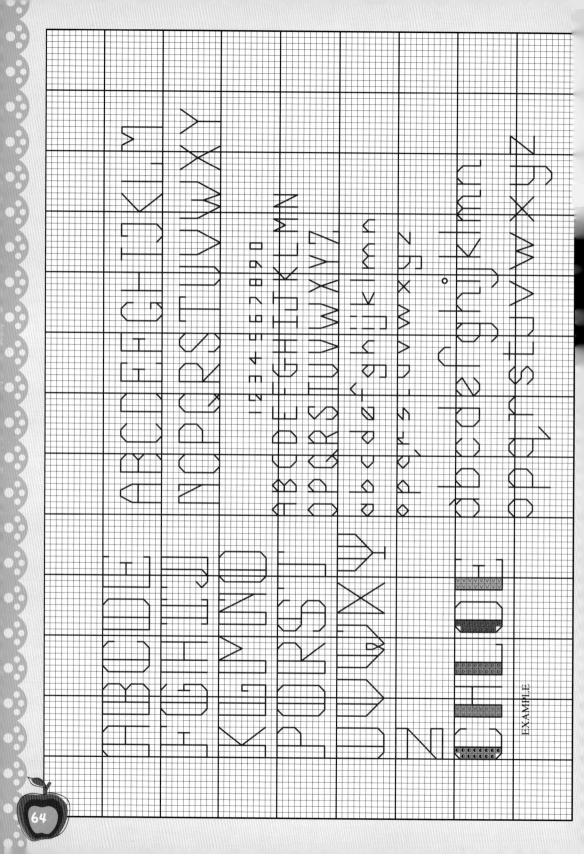